LINUX HACKER'S PRIMER: MASTERING THE BASICS FOR CYBER MASTERY

Contents

Prologue to Linux

1.1 What is Linux?

Linux is an open-source, Unix-like working framework part that fills in as the establishment for different working frameworks (operating system). Initially made by Linus Torvalds in 1991, Linux has developed into a strong and flexible stage. It is important for the more extensive group of free and open-source programming, and its source code can be unreservedly altered, circulated, and utilized.

1.3 Getting and Introducing Linux

Downloading Linux: Most dispersions are accessible free of charge on the web. Visit the authority site of the picked conveyance to download the establishment picture.

Making Media for Installation: Once downloaded, make a bootable USB or DVD from the establishment picture. This can be accomplished with the help of Linux and Windows utilities like dd.

Establishment Interaction: Boot your PC from the establishment media and adhere to the on-screen directions. You'll regularly have to pick a language, segment your plate, set up a client account, and design the framework.

Post-Installation: After establishment, you might have to refresh the framework, introduce extra programming, and design settings in light of your inclinations.

Key Learning's:

Linux is an open-source working framework part.
Linux dispersions give total, easy to use working frameworks worked around the Linux bit.
Different circulations take care of various inclinations and use cases.
The establishment cycle includes downloading a picture, making establishment media, and designing the framework.

Basics of the Command Line: Terminal and Shell Terminal:

The terminal is a text-based interface in which you collaborate with the working framework. You can use it to run commands, navigate the file system, and do other things.

Shell: The user's input is processed by the shell, which is a command interpreter. Normal shells incorporate Slam (Bourne Again SHell), Zsh, and Fish.

2.2 The pwd (Print Working Directory) Basic Commands:

Shows the ongoing working index.

(List): bash Copy code pwd ls Records documents and catalogs in the ongoing registry.

ls cd (Change Directory) in bash: Changes the ongoing working catalog.

slam
Duplicate code
cd/way/to/index
cp (Duplicate): Duplicates documents or catalogs.

slam
Duplicate code
cp source objective
mv (Move): Moves or renames records or indexes.

slam
Duplicate code
mv source objective
rm (Eliminate): Erases records or registries.

slam

Duplicate code
rm record

2.3 Record and Index Control

mkdir (Make Registry): Makes another registry.

slam
Duplicate code
mkdir new_directory
rmdir (Eliminate Catalog): removes a directory that is empty.

bash: Copy code, rmdir, and touch: Makes an unfilled document or updates the timestamp of a current record.

slam
Duplicate code
contact filename
feline (Connect): Shows the items in a document.

slam
Duplicate code
feline filename
nano or vim: Content tools for making or altering documents.

slam
Duplicate code
nano filename

2.4 Consents and Proprietorship

chmod (Change Mode): Changes document authorizations.

slam
Duplicate code
chmod authorizations filename
chown (Change Proprietor): Changes record possession.

slam
Duplicate code

chown proprietor: filename group
sudo (Superuser Do): Executes an order with superuser honors.

slam
Duplicate code
sudo order
Key Focus points:

The terminal is the text-based interface for communicating with the working framework.
Normal shells incorporate Slam, Zsh, and Fish.
Essential orders incorporate pwd, ls, disc, cp, mv, and rm.
Commands for manipulating files and directories include mkdir, rmdir, touch, cat, nano, and vim.
Consents and possession can be overseen utilizing chmod, chown, and sudo.

Organizing Stray pieces

3.1 IP Regions and Subnetting

IP Address: An inventive numerical number relegated to every gadget associated with a PC association is known as an IP address. It fills two boss necessities: host or affiliation interface ID and district tending to.

IPv4 Model: 192.168.0.1 IPv6 Framework: Subnetting: 2001:0db8:85a3:0000:0000:8a2e:0 370:7334 Subnetting integrates secluding an IP network into sub-relationship to encourage execution and security moreover. It maintains and enhances network resources.

3.2 Ifconfig or IP for the Association Plan:

plans and demonstrates network interfaces.

ifconfig ping: duplicate code slam Tests network openness.

ping example.com traceroute: slam Duplicate code reveals the path that packs must follow in order to reach a goal.

hammer
Duplicate code
traceroute example.com
netstat: displays information about the network, such as open ports.

hammer
Duplicate code
netstat - an

course: Shows and controls the IP organizing table.

nslookup or dig:

3.3 Investigating Organization Issues

Convert region names to IP addresses with slam Duplicate code course - n

hammer
Duplicate code
nslookup example.com
tcpdump: Gets and isolates network traffic.

hammer
Duplicate code
sudo tcpdump - I eth0
iptables: Sorts out the Linux part firewall.

sudo iptables - L nmap: Slam Duplicate Code looks for administrations and open ports in an organization.

hammer Copy code for nmap - p 1-100 example.com Important actions:

IP addresses wonderfully perceive gadgets on an affiliation.
Subnetting isolates networks for better asset the board and security.
The orders ifconfig, ping, traceroute, netstat, and course are irrefutably used for network plan.
Looking at instruments unite nslookup or dig, tcpdump, iptables, and nmap.

Understanding the File System Root Directory (/):

File System Hierarchy 4.1 The high level registry in the Linux document framework.

It organizes all of the other directories and files below it.

container (Parallel): Contains fundamental double executables (orders) for the framework.

and so forth((Setup Documents): Stores framework wide design documents and shell scripts.

home: Home registries for client accounts are situated here.

lib (Library): consists of shared libraries that system programs require.

usr (Client): Secondary hierarchy for program files and user data that can only be read.

Variable: var data that is variable, like spool files and logs.

tmp (Brief): used for files that are only temporary and can be deleted between reboots.

4.2 Key Indexes

/and so on:

Contains setup documents.
Example: /and so on/network/for network-related setups.
/bin:

Fundamental paired executables.
Example: /canister/ls for the ls order.

/home:

Home catalogs for clients.
Example: /home/username/.
/lib and /lib64:

Shared libraries.
Example: /lib/libc.so.6.
/usr:

Auxiliary order for read-just client information.
Example: /usr/container/for client parallels.

4.3 Using the CD (Change Directory) to Navigate the File System:

changes location to the specified directory.

ls (List): bash Copy code cd /path/to/directory   Records documents and catalogs in the ongoing registry.

ls pwd (Print Working Directory): bash Copy code Shows the ongoing working index.

slam
Duplicate code
pwd
cp (Duplicate): Duplicates documents or catalogs.

slam
Duplicate code
cp source objective
mv (Move): Moves or renames records or indexes.

slam
Duplicate code
mv source objective

Key Focal points:

The root registry (/) is the high level catalog in Linux.
Fundamental catalogs incorporate/canister,/and so forth,/home,/lib,/usr, and/var.
The/and so forth registry holds setup documents.
Exploring orders incorporate disc, ls, pwd, cp, and mv.

Client and Gathering the executives

5.1 Adding and Overseeing Clients

useradd: Adds another client to the framework.

slam
Duplicate code
sudo useradd username
passwd: Sets or changes the secret phrase for a client.

sudo passwd username userdel: bash Copy code Erases a client account.

slam
Duplicate code
sudo userdel username

usermod: Adjusts client account properties.

slam
Duplicate code
sudo usermod - aG groupname username

5.2 Client Authorizations

chmod (Change Mode): Changes document authorizations.

slam
Duplicate code
chmod authorizations filename
chown (Change Proprietor): Changes record possession.

slam
Duplicate code
chown proprietor: bunch filename

5.3 Gathering the executives

groupadd: Makes another gathering.

slam
Duplicate code
sudo groupadd groupname
groupdel: Erases a gathering.

slam
Duplicate code
sudo groupdel groupname
usermod: Adds a client to a gathering.

slam
Duplicate code
sudo usermod - aG groupname username
gpasswd: Oversees bunch passwords.

slam
Duplicate code

sudo gpasswd - a username groupname

Key Focal points:

useradd adds another client, passwd sets or changes the secret word, and userdel erases a client.

usermod changes client properties, like gathering enrollment.

chmod changes record authorizations, and chown changes document possession.

groupadd makes another gathering, groupdel erases a gathering, and usermod adds a client to a gathering.

gpasswd oversees bunch passwords.

Cycles and Administrations

6.1 Overseeing Cycles

ps (Cycle Status): Showcases data about dynamic cycles.

slam
Duplicate code
ps
top: Continuous framework observing device.

slam
Duplicate code
top
kill: Ends a cycle by conveying a message.

slam
Duplicate code
kill PID

pkill: Kills or sign cycles in view of their name.

slam
Duplicate code
pkill process_name
killall: Kills processes by name.

slam
Duplicate code
killall process_name

6.2 Observing Framework Assets

free: Showcases how much free and utilized framework memory.

slam
Duplicate code
free
df (Circle Free): Shows plate space utilization.

slam

Duplicate code
df - h
du (Circle Utilization): Shows the size of an index and its items.

slam
Duplicate code
du - h/way/to/registry

6.3 Beginning and Halting Administrations

systemctl: Controls the systemd framework and administration director.

slam
Duplicate code
sudo systemctl start service_name
systemctl stop: Stops a help.

slam
Duplicate code
sudo systemctl stop service_name

systemctl restart: Restarts a help.

slam
Duplicate code
sudo systemctl restart service_name
systemctl empower: Empowers a help to begin on boot.

slam
Duplicate code
sudo systemctl empower service_name
systemctl incapacitate: Cripples a help from beginning on boot.

slam
Duplicate code
sudo systemctl handicap service_name
Key Focus points:

ps shows process data, and top gives constant framework observing.

kill ends an interaction by PID, while pkill and killall do as such by name.

free shows memory use, and df and du show circle space data.

systemctl oversees framework administrations, including beginning, halting, restarting, empowering, and handicapping them.

Security Rudiments

7.1 Firewalls and iptables

iptables: A client space utility program that permits a framework head to design the IP parcel channel rules of the Linux portion firewall.

Model: Permit approaching traffic on port 80 (HTTP).

slam
Duplicate code
sudo iptables - An Information - p tcp - - dport 80 - j Acknowledge
Model: Deny approaching traffic from a particular IP address.

slam
Duplicate code
sudo iptables - An Info - s <IP_ADDRESS> - j DROP

Model: Save and apply the iptables rules.

slam
Duplicate code
sudo administration iptables save
sudo administration iptables restart
7.2 SSH and Secure Correspondence

Secure Shell (SSH): A cryptographic organization convention utilized for secure information correspondence, order line login points of interaction, and remote order execution.

Producing SSH Key Pair:

slam
Duplicate code
ssh-keygen - t rsa - b 4096 - C "your_email@example.com"

Replicating Public Key to Server:

slam
Duplicate code
ssh-duplicate   id
username@remote_host
Debilitating   Secret   phrase
Verification (sshd_config):

slam
Duplicate code
sudo   nano/and   so
forth/ssh/sshd_config
Set PasswordAuthentication to
'no'
sudo systemctl restart ssh

7.3 Client Validation

sudo (Superuser Do): Executes an
order with superuser honors.

Adding a client to the sudo bunch:

slam
Duplicate code
sudo usermod - aG sudo username
Arranging sudoers record:

slam
Duplicate code
sudo visudo
Add the accompanying line to allow a client to execute any order with sudo:

slam
Duplicate code
username ALL=(ALL:ALL) ALL
Key Important points:

iptables is utilized for designing the IP parcel channel rules of the Linux part firewall.
SSH gives a protected correspondence convention and is utilized for remote access.

Producing SSH key coordinates and incapacitating secret key verification improve security.

sudo permits clients to execute orders with superuser honors, and its arrangement is overseen through the sudoers record.

Bundle the executives

8.1 Bundle Chiefs (adept, yum, pacman)

Well-suited (High level Bundle Apparatus):

Update Bundle Rundown:

```
slam
Duplicate code
sudo able update
Introduce Bundle:
```

```
slam
Duplicate code
sudo able introduce package_name
Eliminate Bundle:
```

```
slam
Duplicate code
sudo able eliminate package_name
```

Look for Bundle:

slam
Duplicate code
adept inquiry package_name
YUM (Yellowdog Updater, Altered):

Update Bundle Rundown:

sudo yum check-update install package bash copy code

slam
Duplicate code
sudo yum introduce package_name
Eliminate Bundle:

slam
Duplicate code
sudo yum eliminate package_name
Look for Bundle:

Pacman: yum search package_name
bash copy code

Update Bundle Rundown:

slam
Duplicate code
sudo pacman - Sy
Introduce Bundle:

slam
Duplicate code
sudo pacman - S package_name
Eliminate Bundle:

slam
Duplicate code
sudo pacman - R package_name
Look for Bundle:

slam
Duplicate code
pacman - Ss package_name

8.2 Introducing and Refreshing Programming

well-suited:

Introduce/Update All Bundles:
slam
Duplicate code
sudo well-suited update
yum:

Introduce/Update All Bundles:
slam
Duplicate code
sudo yum update
pacman:

Introduce/Update All Bundles:
slam
Duplicate code
sudo pacman - Syu

8.3 Eliminating Programming

able:

yum: sudo apt autoremove bash
copy code

slam
Duplicate code
sudo yum autoremove
pacman:

slam
Duplicate code
sudo pacman - Rns $(pacman -
Qdtq)
Key Focus points:

The commands for managing
packages differ between package
managers.
In Debian/Ubuntu, Red Hat/Fedora,
and Arch Linux-based systems,
respectively, APT, YUM, and

Pacman are commonly utilized package managers.

Orders incorporate refreshing the bundle list, introducing, eliminating, and looking for bundles.

Overhauling all bundles and eliminating unused conditions upgrade framework effectiveness.

Prearranging Nuts and bolts

9.1 Prologue to slam prearranging

Slam Content Record:

Make a new file for the script:

```
slam
Duplicate code
contact myscript.sh
```

Open the content record in a word processor:

```
slam
Duplicate code
nano myscript.sh
Kit n kaboodle (#!):
```

Begin the content document with a kit n kaboodle line to determine the translator.
slam
Duplicate code
#! /receptacle/slam

9.2 Composing Basic Contents

Factors:

Announce and involve factors in scripts.
slam
Duplicate code
name="John"
reverberation "Hi, $name!"
Client Information:

Scripts can read input from users.
slam
Duplicate code
reverberation "Enter your name:"
understand name

reverberation "Hi, $name!"
Restrictive Proclamations:

Use if, elif, and else for contingent articulations.
slam
Duplicate code
if ["$name" == "John"]; then, at that point,
  reverberation "Hi, John!"
elif ["$name" == "Jane"]; After that, repeat, "Hello, Jane!"
else
  reverberation "Hi, stranger!"
fi 9.3 Automation Using Loops and Scripts:

Use for and keeping in mind that circles for dull assignments.

slam
Duplicate code
for I in {1..5}; do

```
 reverberation "Emphasis $i"
done
slam
Duplicate code
counter=0
while [ $counter - lt 5 ]; do not
repeat "Counter: $counter"
 ((counter++))
done
```

Capabilities:

Characterize and involve capabilities in scripts.

```
echo "Hello, $1!" using the bash
Copy code function greet()
}

welcome "Alice"
```

Key Focus points:

Slam prearranging includes making and executing Slam scripts.

With a shebang line (#!), begin a script file. /bin/bash).

Scripts can make use of variables, user input, and conditional statements.

Execute circles for redundant undertakings and capabilities for code association.

Scripts robotize undertakings, making them valuable for framework organization and different purposes.

Fundamental Devices for Hacking

10.1 Nmap for Organization Checking

Introduce Nmap:

slam
Duplicate code
sudo well-suited introduce nmap # For Debian/Ubuntu
sudo yum introduce nmap # For Red Cap/Fedora
sudo pacman - S nmap # For Curve Linux
Fundamental Sweep:

slam
Duplicate code
nmap target_ip
Administration Variant Location:

slam
Duplicate code
nmap - sV target_ip
Operating system Location:

slam
Duplicate code
nmap - O target_ip

10.2 Wireshark for Parcel Investigation

Introduce Wireshark:

slam
Duplicate code
sudo adept introduce wireshark # For Debian/Ubuntu
sudo yum introduce wireshark # For Red Cap/Fedora
sudo pacman - S wireshark # For Curve Linux
Catch Traffic:

slam
Duplicate code
sudo wireshark
Apply Show Channels:

Channel by IP: ip.addr == target_ip
Channel by Convention: tcp, udp, and so forth.

10.3 Metasploit for Abuse

Introduce Metasploit:

Adhere to the guidelines on the authority Metasploit site.
Begin Metasploit Control center:

slam
Duplicate code
msfconsole
Look for Exploits:

slam
Duplicate code

search exploit_type
Utilize an Endeavor:

slam
Duplicate code
use exploit_name
Set Payload and Choices:

slam
Duplicate code
set PAYLOAD payload_type
set RHOSTS target_ip
Execute the Adventure:

slam
Duplicate code
exploit
Key Important points:

Nmap is an integral asset for network checking, administration rendition location, and operating system recognition.

Wireshark is utilized for catching and investigating network parcels.

Metasploit is an infiltration testing structure that gives an assortment of exploits, payloads, and helper modules for security testing and hacking purposes.

Note: Consistently guarantee that you have the essential consents and are working inside lawful and moral limits while involving devices for security testing or hacking. Unapproved utilization of these apparatuses is unlawful and dishonest.

Web Fundamentals for Programmers

11.1 Figuring out Web Conventions

HTTP (Hypertext Move Convention):

The underpinning of information correspondence on the Internet. It characterizes how messages are arranged and sent.
HTTPS (Hypertext Move Convention Secure):

The safe rendition of HTTP that encodes information during transmission utilizing SSL/TLS.
DNS (Space Name Framework):

Settle space names to IP addresses.

11.2 Apparatuses for Web Application Testing

Burp Suite:

A web application security testing toolbox, utilized for checking, slithering, and breaking down web applications.
OWASP ZAP (Zed Assault Intermediary):

An open-source security testing device for tracking down weaknesses in web applications.
Nikto:

A web server scanner that distinguishes potential security issues.

11.3 Taking advantage of Web Weaknesses

SQL Infusion:

Controlling SQL inquiries to acquire unapproved admittance to a data set.
slam
Duplicate code
' OR '1'='1'; - -
Cross-Site Prearranging (XSS):

Infusing malevolent contents into website pages saw by different clients.
html
Duplicate code
<script>alert('XSS')</script>
Cross-Site Solicitation Phony (CSRF):

Constraining a client to perform undesirable activities without their assent.
html
Duplicate code

```
<img
src="https://example.com/transfer
?amount=1000&to=hacker_account
"/>
```

Index Crossing:

Getting to documents and indexes outside the web root.
slam
Duplicate code

```
../../../../../and so on/passwd
```

Key Focus points:

Understanding web conventions like HTTP, HTTPS, and DNS is significant for web application testing.

Devices like Burp Suite, OWASP ZAP, and Nikto help with checking and recognizing weaknesses.

Taking advantage of weaknesses like SQL infusion, XSS, CSRF, and catalog crossing requires cautious comprehension of web application security. Continuously perform security testing morally and with legitimate approval.

Conclusion

This guide has provided an overview of essential Linux commands, the fundamentals of networking, the file system hierarchy, user and group management, processes and services management, security fundamentals, package management fundamentals, scripting fundamentals, and fundamental hacking tools. Featuring a couple of central issues is significant:

- Responsible Use: Hacking devices and strategies examined in this guide are intended for instructive and moral purposes. Unapproved and pernicious utilization of these instruments is unlawful and deceptive.

- Nonstop Learning: The universe of Linux and network protection is immense and steadily advancing. Continuous education is necessary to maintain relevance and effectiveness.

- Security Attitude: It is essential to Figure out the rudiments of safety. Continuously focus on security while setting up and overseeing frameworks. Consistently update programming, arrange firewalls, and follow best practices to safeguard against likely dangers.

- Lawful and Moral Contemplations: Continuously guarantee you have legitimate approval prior to endeavoring any security testing or hacking exercises. Unapproved admittance to frameworks or organizations is a serious offense.

- Collaboration and community: Draw in with the network safety local area, take part in discussions, and team up with similar people. The advancement of the cybersecurity field is aided by the exchange of experiences and knowledge.

- Keep in mind, the abilities examined in this guide can be applied in different settings, from framework organization and programming improvement to moral hacking and online protection. Move toward these points with a feeling of obligation, continuously keeping lawful and moral guidelines.